In Him I Live!

Treasures from My Heart
Poetry for God's Beloved

Nadine Flowers

PriorityONE
p u b l i c a t i o n s
Detroit, Michigan, USA

*Priority*ONE Publications
P. O. Box 725 • Farmington, MI 48332
(800) 331-8841 Nationwide Toll Free
E-mail: info@p1pubs.com
URL: http://www.p1pubs.com

ISBN: 1-933972-08-4

Cover and interior design *by Christina Dixon*

Printed in the United States of America

Dedication

This book is dedicated to my late parents, who loved, guided, encouraged and molded me into the person I am today. They always wanted the best for me and sacrificed so that I could have the opportunities necessary to excel in life.

My mom was the mother who was always there for me and always had my best interests at heart. She was my support system and I could talk to her about anything. I will always remember my dad as a strong, loving and dedicated father and family man. Against all odds he stood tall and overcame many obstacles in life. His compassion and sacrifice for others has been a light on my pathway of life, showing me how to love others God's way.

Thank you mom and dad for being the loving parents you were and for the wonderful memories that will forever be in my heart.

Mom, 1928-1993
Dad, 1928-2008

Acknowledgments

First and foremost, I thank God for placing this gift in me and for what He has done in my life. As I look back on my experiences, I know that He has had His hand on me all of my life.

I would like to acknowledge the following people for inspiring and encouraging me in writing this book: my daughters, Sherice and Nataki Bluford, James, Dorysse and Francis Bluford, my brother, Jerry L. Flowers, my sisters, Maxine Glenn and Debby Sims, Bishop Isaac King and Pentecostal Temple C.OG.I.C., where I received my foundation in holiness and inspiration for many of the tributes and dedications at Pentecostal Temple.

I also thank Marla Larkin who provided me with the opportunity to share some of my poems with others and Sherry Neal, who has several of my poems because she enjoyed my writing and consistently encouraged me to go to the next level. Gloria Alexander, Ruth Washington, Betty Rozier and Cynthia Knight who critiqued many of my poems before anyone else saw them. Pat Johnson-Taylor and Gwen Bingham inspired and encouraged me before I began to get serious about writing.

I also acknowledge my pastor, Dr. James L. Morman, and Christian Tabernacle Church where I continue to learn and grow in the grace and knowledge of Jesus Christ.

I thank God for the people He has placed in my life, with whom I have built precious relationships and have helped to shape and mold me and make me a better person.

Table of Contents

Tributes: Family & Friends

In Loving Memory

Notable Mix

Preface

In this life we will encounter many obstacles, trials and tribulations. Yet, there are revelations and insights to the benefits of loving, knowing, trusting and having God as Head of your life. When we know and trust Him, no matter what we go through, we are victorious.

This book is a collection of writings and poems dating back many years. Some were written during the times when my children were small and others were written throughout my college years up to this present time. The poem, "David - God's Chosen King," was written as part of a college assignment and is one of my favorites.

I believe those who read my book will be encouraged by its messages and inspiration. I believe that once people read this book they will find themselves returning to its pages to lift their spirits and at times they will even direct others to its contents. I believe God wants people to have this book in their hands to help them find the words to express the joys and tribulations of their own hearts, when words won't come.

May this book be a blessing and encouragement to all who read it.

In Him I live and move and have my being.
Acts 17:28

IT'S ALL ABOUT GOD

IN HIM

In Him I am complete.
In Him I have peace.
In Him there is no defeat.

In Him I have all things.
In Him I am redeemed.

In Him I am whole.
In Him I am as pure gold.

In Him I live.
In Him I give.

In Him I move.
In Him I cannot lose.
It is Him that I choose.

In Him there's unspeakable joy.
In Him I praise and lift my voice.

In Him my life is full.
I know Him, He is good!

In this was manifested the love of God toward us,
because that God sent his only begotten Son into the world,
that we might live through him. I John 4:9

MY STEPS ARE ORDERED

Many years ago, before I was born, God had already predestined my life. He created me and placed me in this universe, this time and this space that would be mine. He had a specific purpose for me on this earth that only I could fulfill.

For I know the plans I have for you declares the Lord, plans to prosper you and not to harm you, plans to give you hope and a future. Jeremiah 29:11

He began by giving me two loving parents from humble beginnings in the south. God blessed my parents with three more children to love and share my space, my life and time. My father had always dreamed of a better life for his family and decided to move to Michigan (God places dreams in our hearts to get us to the places we need to be in life). This was a big undertaking for a man with little education but it was an opportunity to earn a better income and provide an education for his children. My steps were being ordered… I would leave the place of my birth to go many miles away. God had a plan for me and it would take me to Michigan. A place where I would grow up and one day learn to know Him personally.

Nothing great, no one special
Just a willing, yielding vessel.
Chosen by God to do His will
wherever He leads me to fulfill.
I can't say I have done great things.
But through His Son I've been redeemed.
He has a plan for my life I know.
And where He leads me I will go.

While growing up, our family endured many struggles. There came a time when my mother's health began to fail. She was a praying woman who loved God and praying for people. Times were hard and there were many days when my father didn't know how he would make ends meet, but God brought us through it all. God called my mother home in 1993. As I look back, I remember how He used other people to bless us in our time of need, just as He does today.

I can run to Him, He's a strong tower.
I can run to Him, He is my strength, my power.
I can run to Him, He is my peace.
I can run to Him and find relief.
I can run to Him, He is my joy.
I can run to Him, to His outstretched arms.
I can run to Him…He waits for me.

I thank God for my space in this time and in this universe. I consider each day a gift and an opportunity to be the willing vessel He uses to do His will in my life. As He orders my steps, I seek to grow in His grace and knowledge each day until He calls me back to Him.

STAND ON THE WORD

How can I stand on the Word?

S   Study the Word

T   Talk the Word

A   Abide in the Word

N   Never doubt the Word

D   Do the Word

I stand up for Jesus because He laid down His life for me!

*Thy word is a lamp to my feet and a light
to my pathway. Psalm 119:105*

GLORIOUS PRAISE

Glorious praise, sincere praise.
Praise so powerful it beckons God to come in,

To dwell and commune with His people.
Praise so sweet, like a fragrance in His nostrils.

Praise like a cloud, lifts my burdens
carrying me to a place of peace and joy.

Glorious praise, an unnatural weapon
against the cares of this world.

Leading me in to the arms of my heavenly Father,
Who encompasses me with His unconditional love.

Praise that takes me into worship of my creator,
Who destined my path before I was born.

Who created me to praise Him in His magnificence,
His glory, His excellence…so awesome, so mighty.

The keeper of my soul, the source of my joy.
His blood, my hope. His love, my life.

Glorious praise in my spirit, in my mouth,
in my feet…in my heart, in my soul.

They will speak of the glorious splendor of your majesty
and meditate on your wonderful works. Psalm 145:5

DAVID-GOD'S CHOSEN KING

David was born in Bethlehem,
Chosen by God to rule the land

As a shepherd boy he tended sheep
While God laid plans for Saul's defeat.

As time went by, God paved the way.
He sent him to Saul's palace to play.

With his harp he soothed Saul's mind,
The only relief that Saul could find.

Then one day Goliath came.
"No one can defeat me!" was his claim.

Young David knew with faith in God
To defeat the giant would not be hard.

With slingshot and stone he took his stand
And the news rang out in all the land.

One quick shot and Goliath was dead.
And the rest of the Philistines quickly fled.

Now David's life was about to change.
Soon he was exiled, no home to claim.

While on the run, God kept him safe.
Until it was time for his rightful place.

There are many things that David did wrong
But his love for God was always strong.

He showed this love with thanksgiving and praise
And confessed and repented for his sinful ways.

These qualities about David I truly admire.
He knew it was praise that God desires.

He knew in sin he must repent
And confess those sins the way God meant.

To honor and praise, love and obey.
In pleasing God that's the only way.

To be like Jesus, that's my goal
And to learn from the story David's life has told.

I'm striving each day to get it right.
To do what's pleasing in my God's sight.

Although some times the way gets tight,
I know I have Jesus, He's my light.

Through David's life and the Psalms he wrote,
Through the grace of God and the scriptures I quote

My walk with Jesus won't be in vain
As I learn each day to praise His name!

I took you from the pasture and from following the flock to be
ruler over my people, Israel
I Samuel 7:8

GOD'S HEIRS

In society today to be a King means wealth.
But wealth has no meaning without Christ, He's our help.

A Queen brings to mind a beautiful face
But when we have Christ we have beauty and grace.

The very first King had no wealth or fame.
Chosen by God to glorify His name.

True wealth does not come from worldly possessions
But from loving everyone through Christ's intercessions.

Prince or Princess, King or Queen.
A title of stature and self-esteem.

As God's children we're heirs to the throne
Of the greatest King ever known.

The King of Kings, Christ who died
And in His love we can abide.

One day heaven our ultimate goal.
No more sin to tempt our souls.

We have a reason to hold our heads high
For we have a gift money can't buy.

Our gift from God, eternal life,
to live in peace, free from strife.

We're all kings and queens, sisters and brothers.
Jesus just wants us to love one another.

*Listen my dear brothers has God not chosen those who are poor
in the eyes of the world to be rich in faith and to inherit the
Kingdom He promised those who love Him? James 2:5*

SOMEONE

There is someone who's always there.
And you can call on Him anywhere.

Any time of day no special place.
Just call His name and seek His face.

Unconditional love you can come as you are.
No task or feat is ever too hard.

He gave His life that we may live.
What greater gift can anyone give?

One day He came to save the world.
Every man, every woman, every boy and girl.

He walked among us to show us the way.
So we could be with Him in heaven one day.

His name is Jesus, He's waiting for you
To accept Him and know Him but you must choose.

Long ago the Lord said to Israel:
"I have loved you, my people, with an everlasting love.
With unfailing love I have drawn you to myself. Jeremiah 31:3

THE BOOK

I have love and knowledge that overflows
Within my pages the universe begins and ends—just like man.

Comfort, peace, and love is what I am.
Pages of experience
From the beginning of time.

A guide, for man
To conquer life's daily experiences.

I hold the answer to eternal life.
The answer to the problems of mankind.

The way the truth and the life.
I AM THE BIBLE, THE BOOK OF ALL BOOKS.

So why do I sit on a shelf
collecting dust

when everything you need
is here?!

*But **grow** in **grace**, and in the knowledge of our Lord and
Savior Jesus Christ. II Peter 3:17*

THE WORD

The word of God will never change.
Yesterday, today, tomorrow the same.

It never fails its forever true.
It makes, molds and changes you.

Your heart can be changed and your mind renewed
If you focus on God and not your own views.

He gave us His word, it's the bible you know,
To show us the way and direction to go.

To renew your mind you must study His word.
Because there are many who have not heard.

Whatever we need from day to day
is in the bible but we must also pray.

We all need a personal relationship with God,
Learning and seeking with a sincere heart.

His word says seek Him while He may be found.
He can loose those shackles and turn your life around.

For the word of the LORD is right and true;
he is faithful in all he does.
Psalm 33:4

THE HOLY GHOST, THE INDISPENSABLE POWER

Power. What is it? How is it defined?
It's a weapon for change for all mankind.

Authority, ability, influence, control.
This is the power the Holy Ghost holds.

No greater gift bestowed on man.
God gave it freely that we'd understand.

We are His children He commands us to love.
Never envying one another, never holding a grudge.

Hospitality and love should be our goal.
Doing good to all people and praying for souls.

Walk in the spirit, abide in the Vine
Allowing the light of Jesus to shine.

To be good and faithful, gentle and kind,
Crucifying flesh, leaving sin behind.

To have patience and temperance, joy and peace
But most of all, love that will never cease.

Our souls should bear fruit, He walked it first.
Jesus, our example, He died for us.

The Holy Ghost today as in Pentecost remains;
Our gift from heaven and our weapon for change.

But you will receive power when the Holy Spirit comes on you;
and you will be my witnesses in Jerusalem and in all Judea
and Samaria, and to the ends of the earth." Acts 1:8

TRUE FAITH

God said it is impossible to please Him without faith.
It is tested many times when He tells us to wait.

Our love for Jesus is based on faith.
As we accept Him in our hearts and receive His grace.

Faith can vary, there are different degrees
It may be the size of a mountain or a tiny mustard seed.

Whatever the size, whether large or small,
You'll surely miss God with no faith at all.

Some think they know what faith is all about.
Faith does not consist of worry or doubt.

Faith is hope that cannot be seen,
Confidence in the promises God said He'd bring.

Faith is trust, assurance, belief.
A gift from God everyone should seek.

Faith is a compass that leads us to God.
Uplifting our souls, stirring our hearts.

Faith is power - it can change many things
A benefit of faith is the peace it can bring.

Exercise your faith without works, it is dead.
Stand on His word. He'll do what He said.

Remember, true faith will open the door.
And the promises of God can surely be yours.

*In him and through faith in him we may approach God
with freedom and confidence. Ephesians 3:12*

LORD LIFT ME HIGHER

Lord lift me higher, help me to grow.
Show me the way to praise you more.

I need you Lord, each day each hour.
You are my refuge, my strength, my power.

I want to walk closer to be more like You
To serve You, love You, to glorify You.

Teach me to pray in every way
To seek your face every day.

Use me Lord to do Your will,
Living my life the way I should live.

I want others to see You in me.
To know that through You they can be free.

Help me be all You want me to be
To do good deeds, to sow good seeds.

Lord You died to save me from sin.
And I know on you I can always depend.

Show me your ways, O LORD, teach me your paths; Psalm 25:4

THANK YOU JESUS

Thank you Jesus for loving me so.
Thank you Jesus for letting me know.

Thank you Jesus, You died for me.
Thank you Jesus for setting me free.

Thank you Jesus for the birds and trees.
Thank you Jesus for the rivers and streams.

Thank you Jesus for the grass so green.
Thank you Jesus for visions and dreams.

Thank you Jesus, You made me see.
Thank you Jesus, You're the One for me.

Thank you Jesus for the bright sunshine.
Thank you Jesus because I know You're mine.
Thank you Jesus for Your mercy and grace.

Thank you Jesus for each day I face.
When I think of You Jesus all I can do

Is thank You and thank You for wonderful You!

*It is good to praise the Lord and make music
to your name O most High Psalm 91:2*

THIS TEMPLE

God gave me this temple - it's mine for a while.
He did it because He loves me and I am His child.

While I have this temple I am never to abuse it.
I must treat it with care and never misuse it.

There's no other like this one, none are the same
This temple was made just to glorify His name.

He gave me these hands to help others and to give
He gave me this heart to love and forgive.

Lips to encourage and tell others the news
of His goodness and love that it's Him they should choose.

These legs and feet to go near or far,
showing love to others whomever they are.

These ears are to hear Him instruct me in His way
To know He is with me every day.

Eyes to see and read His word
Giving Him the glory He deserves.

Because in this temple the Holy Spirit resides
He's cherished and precious you see, He's my guide.

So as long as I live I must never forget.
God gave me this temple so His name would be blessed!

Do you not know that your body is a temple of the Holy Spirit,
who is in you, whom you have received from God? You are not your own;
I Corinthians 6:19

HE'S THERE FOR YOU

When things happen that we don't understand
And we've prayed and prayed for the move of God's hand.

His word says trust Him, have faith and believe
He'll bring you out if you let Him lead.

Yes, trials will come and trials will go
But through it all one thing I know

The word of God is forever and true
It accomplishes all it says it will do.

Remember when you're going through
God is just making and molding you.

So do not fear, do not fret.
He'll carry you through each trial and test.

The Lord himself goes before you and will be with you;
He will never leave you nor forsake you. Do not be afraid; do not be discouraged.
Deuteronomy 31:8

WHAT CAN I RENDER?

What can I render for his benefits to me?
The sacrifice of praise and my availability.

What can I render to someone so great?
The One who created me for His name's sake.

What can I render for all He's done?
But to be an example in the image of His Son.

What can I do that is pleasing in His eyes?
But seek His face and in His word abide.

What can I do but to lift up His name?
Offering my praise without guilt or shame.

What can I render for His goodness, His grace?
But thanksgiving and worship for the rest of my days.

*Therefore, I urge you brothers, in view of God's mercy
to offer your bodies as living sacrifices, holy and pleasing
to God, this is your spiritual act of worship. Romans 12:1*

ME

I am me, God made me.
Just as I am, like no other.

No one can do
what God created me to do.

I am like no other, I am me.
No other can I be.

I must be me
because God made me
free to be me!

I am me, God knows my name.
My steps are ordered
My life ordained.

I am me and He's there for me.
He loves me and guides me
He's my destiny.

I am me, He cares for me.
There's no one like Him.
He made me!

For you created my inmost being;
you knit me together in my mother's womb.
Psalm 139:13

CREATED TO PRAISE

Created to praise that's the reason we're here,
to praise God's name and draw Him near.

It's in His praise that He comes in
to dwell with us and cleanse us again.

Our praise is sweet, it's His desire.
It honors Him and lifts us higher.

We are to praise Him all day long,
in good times and bad and when things go wrong.

A praise on our lips in song or prayer.
In instruments and dance, His word says to wear it.

A praise that is glorious, sweet and great.
A praise that is true, sincere, and not fake.

Giving to God the glory He deserves.
Yes, giving Him the praise as commanded in His Word.

Keeping a praise in our hearts and minds
Will lift our burdens, leaving worry behind.

Praise is the answer to worry and defeat
If we remember to praise Him, His blessings we'll reap.

The people I formed for myself that they may proclaim my praise.
Isaiah 43:21

LIFE IS A JOURNEY

CHOOSE YOUR DESTINY

Our choices determine our destiny. We must be careful about the choices we make because they can be with us for a lifetime. The decisions we make are based on our individual experiences, environment, and personality. People with positive attitudes are happier, healthier, and more successful. I believe positive people smile a lot and smiles are contagious. Negativity and inflexibility will inhibit the opportunity for growth and diversity in our lives.

A positive attitude is the key to overcoming any circumstance we encounter. We can choose the outcome we desire in life by maintaining a positive attitude, setting goals and acting on them. In times of adversity, seek God for direction. He is in control. Sometimes it is not easy to give it to God because not being in control of a situation gives way to worry and anxiety. Releasing our problems to God will result in the peace of God.

When the storms of life are blowing your way, never give up. Seek God, trust Him to handle the situation and don't compare yourself to others. God gave us our own unique set of gifts and talents that distinguish us from anyone else. Use those gifts, maintain a positive attitude and make the right choices.

DECISIONS

Daily decisions are a way of life
Whatever we do we have a choice.

Some are routine, not given much thought.
Others are life changing, some stressful, some not.

From the time we wake up and all day long
There are never ending choices we must make on our own.

It's relatively simple to choose some things.
A color, a fragrance, a hairdo or shoes;
a shirt or tie or what tool to use.

Then there are others not so easy to choose.
A house, a car, appliance or budget.
Should I intervene in a situation, or just not touch it.

Yes, in this life there are many choices to be made;
but the greatest, most important, is the choice to be saved.

To accept Jesus, He's the greatest friend.
He has joy and peace, life without end.

When you make this choice, you can't go wrong.
Because He'll never leave you on your own.

With Him there's hope and heavenly treasure.
There's no greater joy, no greater pleasure.

So please, don't wait, don't delay,
His arms are open, He's waiting today.

Just confess your sins, repent He'll hear,
Call on Him, He's forgiven you, He's near.

So remember each day when making choices
be sure you've made the important one.

By choosing Jesus you've chosen life,
The way God planned it through His Son.

THE GIFT OF LIFE

Life is so precious, a gift we take for granted.
It holds many mysteries we do not know.

Questions asked, answers sought,
there are things in life that can't be bought.

As we walk this journey we call life,
With all its miseries heartaches and strife,

We must learn there is nothing we own.
What we have is only a loan.

We must remember, God created all.
He built it up and He can make it fall.

The plan is laid out on how to live this life;
how to overcome the heartaches and strife.

If we take hold of the Word of God,
Keeping it always in our minds and hearts;

He promised to keep us through heartaches and pain,
When we're obedient and pray we can call on His name.

LIVE IN LOVE

There are so many things in life we endure.
Broken homes, heartache, diseases with no cure.

Sometimes it seems everything goes wrong.
To get through it all, we must be strong.

Many things happen that we don't understand,
things we can't control, things we never planned.

The world today seems headed for destruction.
Drugs taking over, turmoil is erupting.

There is so much distress, guns, killing, fear, unrest.
We need more love to help us progress.

Everyone is unique, God made us that way.
We should learn to love, learn to pray.

Life is so short we should take some time;
show a little love, begin with a smile.
Because we're only here for a little while.

DO WHAT YOU CAN

Do what you can for your fellow man.
Love and cherish him while you can.

Tomorrow is not promised to us, you know.
We all have a time we must go.

When the time has come and my life is done.
I want no regrets from anyone,

I hope I can say I did my best,
to make someone happy, no more no less.

Let no one say, "if only I'd tried";
to do a little more while she was alive.

Do all you can for your fellow man.
Make someone happy while you still can.

'Cause when life is done and the person is gone,
what you wish you had done will never be known.

9/11 - WHAT TIME IS IT?

It's time to wake up, open our eyes and see.
The freedom we take for granted may be impossible to keep.

It's time to wake up, open our eyes and see.
Destruction taking place all around you and me.

It's time to wake up, time to make a change.
Life from now on will never be the same.

It's time to wake up, kneel down and pray.
Ask God to heal our nation and guide us day by day.

It's time to wake up and turn to God above.
He's the one to save us and teach us how to love.

It's time to wake up and come together as one
Praying to God that His will be done.

It's time to wake up, leave this path of destruction
With self imposed agendas of greed and corruption.

It's time to wake up, all the signs are here
Time is getting shorter, the end is near.

It's time to wake up, look at the clock and the hour
We'd better prepare or be devoured.

What time is it?
IT'S WAKE UP TIME!

OUR FALLEN OFFICERS

We honor all Officers who bravely gave their lives;
serving the community and nation with dedication and pride.

We honor the fallen Officers who paid the price,
to protect each citizen and preserve their rights.

We honor those Officers who walked the beat,
working long hours without much sleep.

People dying, mothers crying,
drug dealers selling, addicts buying.

Those who monitored, accosted and chased,
a never ending war they willingly faced.

We honor the fallen Officers on the battlefield,
enforcing the law against criminals who lie, cheat and kill.

We honor the fallen Officers who died that we'd be free.
We cannot take for granted what they did for you and me.

We honor the fallen Officer who was a father, son, or brother,
the one who was someone's sister, daughter, or mother.

We won't forget those Officers, Soldiers, and Vets.
No way can we repay them, we're forever in their debt.

So today we come together, our hearts and purpose one,
to commemorate the memory of those who fought and won!

REBIRTH

Spring is a beautiful time of year.
As a rebirth pattern unfolds so clear.

What happens in spring is a glorious sight.
So many things growing under God's sun light.

Green grass, green leaves and budding trees.
Pretty butterflies and honey bees.

Nature gives us a miraculous show,
As she nurtures and allows her children to grow

Flowers so beautiful that smell so sweet.
All signs of spring that nature repeats.

If you look closer you will find,
there's rebirth around us of every kind.

Politics, religion, and art are a few.
This rebirth pattern is a part of you.

Life can bring happiness, disappointment too.
But the rebirth pattern is life renewed.

CHANGE–A FACT OF LIFE

Change and diversity, a fact of life.
Viewed by some as a challenge and to others as strife.

How's your attitude when it comes to change?
Do you fight and resist, murmur and complain?

Wherever you go or whatever you do,
there's an encounter with change waiting for you.

You cannot avoid it and no one is exempt,
But a positive attitude should be your intent.

The definition of change is to alter or replace.
It's an event that's constant and cannot be erased.

Diversity and variety creates interest and fun.
It assists some of us in getting the job done.

Well-planned decisions can bring positive results.
With enormous benefits not based on luck.

When we choose to embrace those times of change,
We find growth and progress and much to gain.

So whatever the change we encounter these days,
Let's look at the positive and move to the next phase.

If we allow each change to become a stepping stone,
We can use our experiences to build and grow on.

TRUE FRIENDS

WHAT IS A FRIEND?

When you have a true friend you have a rare treasure.
A friend is a gift beyond measure.

A friend is there when you're feeling low.
When you need to talk, to a friend you can go.

A friend will tell you when you're right.
A friend will tell you when you're wrong.

But with a friend you're never alone.
A friend shares good times, bad times, all times.
A friend is there no matter what time.

A friend loves you without apprehension.
Overlooks your faults without contention.

With a friend you can laugh or cry,
But a real friend will never say goodbye.

There may come a time when friends must part.
But true friendship remains forever in the heart.

WHO

F   Who can I count on to make my <u>F</u>rowns disappear?

R   Who can I turn to when times are <u>R</u>ough?

I   Who gives me <u>I</u>nspiration, understanding, trust?

E   Who stands by me from beginning to <u>E</u>nd?

N   Who <u>N</u>ever forgets me through thick and thin?

D   None other than the one on whom I can <u>D</u>epend!

FRIEND!

A BOY CALLED ROE

When I was small, a long time ago,
there was a boy, they called him Roe.

As children we played; we had such fun.
But Roe would play, and then he'd run.

He liked to tease and make me cry;
and when I cried he'd run and hide.

Many years have passed since then.
And now we'll never meet again.

I'd always hoped the day would come
when we'd talk of those days of fun.

I'm told he grew up a caring man,
Always willing to lend a hand.

Whatever he had, he was willing to share.
The compassion he had was beyond compare.

His time on earth was not very long
His life was short and now he's gone.

The memories I have of this boy Roe
are the only memories of him I'll know.

Those memories I'll treasure with one regret.
The man called Roe I never met.

ARE YOU THE ONE?

Can I turn to you for truth and honesty?
Can I lean on you faithfully?

Can I turn to you when times are tough?
For inspiration, understanding, trust?

Will you stand by me until the end?
When I need you will you be there
through thick and thin?

Are you the one on whom I can depend?
The one I can truly call my friend?

CLOSER THAN A BROTHER

The bible says a friend sticks closer than a brother
A friend is there when you have no other.

A friend is one who accepts you as you are
He's truthful and caring with a loving heart.

A friend is trustworthy, a true confidante
A positive influence, your life he'll enhance.

He lifts you up when you're feeling low.
And when you're wrong he lets you know.

We all should have one and be one too.
Just show yourself friendly for a friend that's true.

THREE FRIENDS

Together we've been for many years
We've shared joy, laughter and tears.

It seems like yesterday when we met.
And it's a day we'll never forget.

It's a day we found a friendship so rare,
a friendship so strong the three of us share.

We've grown to know each other so well
and when something's wrong we can always tell.

Eight years we worked side by side
And now a change has come to our lives.

We all must go our separate ways,
with hope for success and brighter days.

Our days of working together must end
But the three of us know we're forever friends.

PAT

Quiet, understanding, warm and kind.
A very special friend of mine.

She understands me, is there for me,
supports me when I'm down.

She's generous and sensitive
I enjoy having her around.

She's thoughtful and remembers things I forget.
She's very unique like no one I've met.

She's small in stature but quiet and wise.
She takes care of herself despite her size.

Always willing to lend a hand.
Ready to help whenever she can.

She reminds me of how blessed we are,
and it's God who has brought us this far.

I'm so blessed to have Pat as a friend.
I hope she feels the same
and our friendship never ends.

GWEN

Gwen is special, a friend of mine.
Someone who's pleasant friendly and kind.

She has the type of personality
That attracts people to her, like honey to a bee.

She's someone I can truly call my friend
Someone on whom I can depend.

She knows me well and when something is wrong
She knows right away it doesn't take long.

She tries very hard to be real tough
But I know her well and it's all a big bluff.

She's warm and sensitive, I know for a fact.
That tough role impression is only an act.

She tries very hard not to let it show
But through the years I've learned, I know.

She's intelligent and ambitious a woman of strength.
Comical and witty but very intense.

I value our friendship it's lasting and true.
Because friends like Gwen are very few.

FOREVER FRIEND

(To Sherry Neal)

Friends are forever, whether near or far.
Friends never forget no matter where they are.

You're a friend I cherish, the times we've shared were great.
The friendship we share is special, one I appreciate.

You've encouraged and guided me, you've helped me to grow.
You've been a blessing to me, more than you know.

I admire your ability, you're understanding and wise;
you spend time with others and impact their lives.

You're intelligent and kind I know you'll succeed;
because you have God and your paths He will lead.

You've made a decision, a life changing decision
and I know you have God's peace;
His love is the only love that will never, ever cease.

I wish you joy, I wish you love and lots of happiness;
but you won't have a problem there because you are
truly blessed!!

FAMILY

FATHER

What is a father to those who love him?
He is a man of respect honor and love.

For he knows his family is God's gift from above.
He is someone who faces whatever may come,

Someone who knows how the battle is won.
In times of trouble he knows what to do.

He's there for his family to see them through.
He knows as a father he has an important role,

To provide for his family is his number one goal.
He spends time with his children to help them grow strong.

He's the king of his castle, the head of his home.
He protects his family in every way.

He guides them with wisdom and teaches them to pray.
Though fathers are different in more ways than one,

The same can be said by daughter or son.
A father is a blessing, he stands tall like a tree,
because father helps make the family complete.

WHAT IS A MOTHER?

Mothers are a gift from God above.
Endowed with strength,
graced with love.

Given to us as a guiding light.
As a mother she knows how to make things right.

She's someone who is always there;
Willing, giving, sharing, and caring.

The special love God gave mother
is beyond compare,
unlike any other.

We appreciate mother.
We honor her today.

The sacrifices she's made
we could never repay.

BABIES ARE A BLESSING

To Vivian

Babies are a blessing from God above,
full of joy, created in love.

I wish you a labor that goes well without strife.
I wish you a baby that's healthy for life.

I wish you happiness and all that it brings
But I wish you God's love above all of these things.

And when your baby becomes an adult
Be sure you've taught her about God and His love.

For when she encounters the things of this world
She'll know she can trust Him, she'll know of His love.

Teach her to pray and communicate with Him.
Teach her to obey and glorify Him.

Teach her to study and know God's Word
And remember He's the One she must serve.

And when she has learned to do these things,
She'll experience the blessings that only God can bring!

SAVE OUR FAMILIES

Family is the foundation of society; the very backbone and structure of our way of life. God created the family so that life could continue from generation to generation. The mother and father were to be examples to our children; nurturing them and teaching them to be responsible and caring adults. The family today has gone astray and is in danger of becoming extinct.

Crime, turbulence, violence, and hate permeate our society today. Our children are not taught good moral values. They are not seeing the love, compassion, and concern for others as we saw it in the past. People are living for today with no concern for the future and no concern for the children and their future.

The criminals are getting younger and younger. Violent crimes are being committed by our children because that's what they see every day. Our children need to be nurtured, loved and taught. They need quality time with two parents. The problems, temptations, and evil today's children face are phenomenal. Evil has its hands on the schools, homes, and television.

As individuals, we can make a positive influence on our children. There are millions of people in the world and God made each one unique. Everyone has a gift to be used in God's kingdom. Everyone has a God ordained purpose.

I pray for a change in the hearts of people, hearts of love and compassion in every one. I pray for the return and reinforcement of our family structure the way God planned it, that we become living examples for our children. If we could learn to love one another in spite of our differences, many of the problems we have in society would go away. Each one of us can touch someone by showing them love, giving a word of encouragement or just supplying a listening ear. I pray my life will be a legacy of love and inspiration for those whom God has placed in my path. I pray that I made a difference in someone's life.

WE'RE EXPECTING TWINS

To Juanita

We're expecting twins and our lives won't be the same.
We have so much to do…choosing baby clothes,
furniture and names.

In just a short while our twins will arrive
to double the joy and happiness in our lives.

Life with twins won't be dull we know.
Two tiny babies to love as we watch them grow.

A boy and girl make a perfect pair.
And two girls are ideal with pink ribboned hair.

Two boys are nice to dress in blue.
We'll take long walks to the park or zoo.

The creation of life is a miracle, it's true.
But a greater miracle is the creation of two.

A MOTHER'S LOVE - LOSS OF A CHILD

A mother's love runs deep and strong.
It helps us all to carry on.

Though things in life sometimes go wrong,
It's mother's love that pushes on.

Through ups and downs, turmoil and grief,
A mother's love will never cease.

When God decides to call her child
She must remember he's hers just for a while.

Our children are given to us on loan,
By God above to call our own.

Our time on earth we do not know
And when He calls, we must go.

Learn to trust Him, His way is best.
Just hold His hand, He'll do the rest.

MY SHADOW

A shadow is a part of you;
it might be seen or blocked from view.

It follows you and is always there.
It likes to do whatever you do.

I have a shadow that's always around.
Never blocked from view
and can always be found.

All day long during work or play,
My constant companion is at my side.

If I sit down, my shadow sits, too,
Doing whatever it sees me do.

The shadow follows me from room to room.
And never gets tired until after noon.

That's when it's time to take a nap.
And my sweet baby girl goes to sleep in my lap.

WITH LOVE, MOM

My Daughter, You are You

It seems like yesterday you were a baby in my arms.
My baby girl, so sweet and warm.

I've watched you grow into a young woman,
You're independent, successful, and strong.

I've watched you set goals and work toward achieving them.
You understand the importance of preparing for success.

There are so many things in life you have yet to experience.
But realize your choices will determine your destiny.
Remember for every action there is a consequence.

In your beliefs you do not stray.
It does not matter what anyone says.

As your mother I've learned to step back and wait
And continue to pray for you every day.

Nataki, there's a part of you so loving and sweet
And then there's a part of you no one can reach.

You are my daughter, determined, intense.
You'll take on anyone to wrought your defense.

Unrelenting, confident, misunderstood....but loved.
You are my child, my beautiful flower.
You are who you are....you are you.

Love, Mom

SHERICE

I love you Sherice, this you know
and sometimes my love will overflow.

At times my efforts you don't understand,
Like trying to direct you toward God's plan.

Mistakes I've made and sometimes still do
Because as your mother, I want the best for you.

Although you're grown with a mind of your own,
It's hard to be silent if I see something wrong.

I must remember to let go and let God.
I cannot do it myself;

So I continue to pray for you each day.
Trusting God, I wait on His help.

For everything there is a reason,
this you must believe.

And when you give your problems to God,
His blessings you will receive.

Things are rarely the way we plan
but God has His purpose;
His way, in His hand.

The time will come when you will see
with God you have the victory.

There's so much in life that we must learn
And Jesus came to teach us.

But we must be <u>willing</u> to conform
and allow Him to reach us.

It's not easy sometimes
and things can get so bad.

Seek the Lord and with His joy,
He can make you glad.

He has joy that's like no other,
He's totally in control.

You must put Him first and learn to love Him,
with your heart, your mind and soul.

I know you don't want to hear me sometimes
but it's only for your good.

Submit to God and do what's right
and it will work out as it should.

I'm not pushing, this came from God
because time is very short.

I hope you receive these words of love
and tuck them in your heart.

With love,
Mom

NATAKI

Nataki, my child, if you only knew
The magnitude of my love for you.

And though I love you with the love of a mother,
God loves you more than could any other.

You were born after I prayed to God.
He knows our needs He knows our hearts.

Jesus is waiting and so am I.
Please don't reject Him give Him your life.

He's waiting for you to take a step.
With arms outstretched He wants to help.

Though things go wrong and at times look dim,
He wants you to know and trust in Him.

I know there are things you don't understand.
Just know that He loves you and it's in <u>His</u> hands.

When you accept Him, things will change.
Your outlook will be different, you won't be the same.

I know you're saying I've heard this before
But it's so important that you hear it once more.

If you would only give Him a try,
you'll find in His Word that He does not lie.

God gave me this message, He has you on His mind.
The world is in trouble, it's perilous times.

I hope you receive these words of love,
by a mother who loves you and from God above.

With love,
Mom

THE GOODNESS OF GOD

Abundant blessings are all around.
The goodness of God is so profound.

If we would listen, look and be still,
We'd hear Him talking, we'd know His will.

If we would take time to seek Him each day,
He's promised to guide us and show us the way.

All He wants is to be first in our lives
but the choice is ours, we must decide.

He won't force us, He gently knocks,
and waits for us to open our hearts.

He's there for us, we're never alone,
through heartaches, pain, sunshine or storms.

He knows each one of His children by name,
He loves and treats them all the same.

He gave His Son so we could live,
No greater gift can anyone give.

Because He died, we are free.
And we have life eternally.

Sherice my child, God loves you, He cares.
I pray for you daily and He hears my prayers.

Yes, Sherice He knows all about you.
He sees your tears and hears your cry.

He's already promised He'll deliver and save you
It's in His word, He cannot lie.

Through it all He's drawing you near
so you can know Him, so you can hear.

God has blessed you
and you're strong, I know.

He made you, created you
and He won't let you go.

Just remember, always trust Him,
though sometimes life looks dim.

He knows what's best and
He's working things out.

Hold on to your faith
and never doubt.

When making decisions, seek God first.
He has the answer, it's in His Word.

Live your life as He says you should.
Your reward will be great because God is good!

With love,
Mom

75

MY DAUGHTER, MY CHILD

My baby you'll always be
my daughter, you're a part of me.

It seems like yesterday you were a baby in my arms.
Now you're a young lady and you have much to learn.

Young and innocent, adult and child.
You'll find life will make you cry sometimes
and life will make you smile.

So many things you'll want to change but must accept;
you'll learn to grow with each challenge
and move on to the next step.

We try to prepare our children as they're growing up
for the trials and tribulations life springs upon us.

As your mother, I attempt the same,
hoping to shelter you from disappointment and pain.

I hope you'll be strong; you must, to survive in this world.
A world without peace, a world in need of love.

Always be yourself, in control of yourself; don't be lead astray.
And you'll find life's best rewards can be yours one day.

There are many temptations which lead us to harm.
At times we must be strong we must be calm.
Strong in our faith that God will see us through and He will not fail.
If we're strong in God, we're strong in ourselves.

Many times we feel our problems are great like a tower
but if we look, there are others with problems greater than ours.

Remember, if we look, we'll find the positive and good
in ourselves, in people, and in life!

With love,
Mom

LOVE & MARRIAGE

THE POWER OF LOVE

Love is a word that is defined in many ways by many people. It is a powerful word and is highly misused and abused. Many things are done in the name of love and some are not love at all. Jesus is God's example of love.

The bible says love is giving of yourself to another. John 3:16 says, "For God so loved the world, that <u>He gave</u> His only begotten Son, that whoever believes in Him should not perish, but have everlasting life." We are <u>commanded</u> to love one another, which means it is an act of the will (John 13:34). It is not based on feeling, but doing. "Love your neighbor as yourself." Giving of your time, your finances, encouragement is an act of love. Love is an action word. Love is doing for others. Love can change the world if it is practiced as God commanded. God is love and He proved it by <u>giving</u> His only begotten Son that we may have eternal life.

Love is the greatest gift bestowed on man. God placed a longing deep down inside of us that can only be satisfied through Him, because God is love. Many people have not been taught the true meaning of love. It goes beyond the physical touch. It is spiritual because it comes from God and some people don't know how to give love or receive it. <u>Give</u> and you will receive. Love and you will be loved.

GOD BLESS OUR MARRIAGE

The love of Jesus has brought us together.
He's given us this day to share forever.

Through His love, our love has grown as a flower.
We ask Him to join us with His anointing power.

To make this marriage a marriage of three,
to always be with us, to help us succeed.

We ask Him to always be the head of our lives,
knowing in Him, we can always confide.

We ask Him to guide us, with His loving hand,
to help us be patient when we don't understand.

To help us pray, each and every day
to acknowledge Him always in every way.

To give us strength wherever we're weak,
knowing in Him there is no defeat.

To help us grow strong in Him, together
with wisdom and knowledge, any storm we will weather.

To help us encourage and cherish each other
as a friend, sister, brother and lover.

Lord, help us keep our focus on You
storing treasures in heaven as you told us to do.

Lord, we owe it all to You
and to You we give the glory and praise.

We pray for your presence, we pray for your strength
We pray you'll be with us for the rest of our days.

UNCONDITIONAL LOVE

Unconditional love is God's command;
His example was Jesus, who walked with man.

The instructions are written, it's there in His Word;
He's given us teachers so it can also be heard.

If we hear and apply it to our lives each day,
It all comes back if we just give it away.

It requires loving others, just as they are,
To the unkind, unlovable we must open our hearts.

Love your neighbor as yourself.
Not based on feelings, this must be kept.

Love is the greatest command there is.
Love is carried out whenever we give.

Not always money, but of ourselves, our time,
a word of encouragement and just being kind.

Yes, unconditional love, God expects from us
And it's never hard if we put Him first.

A NEW THRESHOLD OF LIFE

Soon you will cross a new threshold in life.
A new way of life unlike before.
You'll need courage, strength and a whole lot more.

Being married to someone is not an easy task.
Be ready and be strong if you want it to last.

This is the time when you must grow up,
because it takes two to make a marriage work.

Instead of yourself there will be another.
Not always you, you must think of each other.

Don't be selfish, be understanding,
Kind and loving, not demanding.

There will be good times and there will be bad times;
But your love for God and one another
will see you through all times.

Remember this verse as a favor to me,
"Whoso trusteth in the Lord, happy is he" (*Proverbs 16:20*).
Be happy, be loving and be forever.

ORDAINED TO BE WIVES

God made woman especially for man.
From the very beginning she was part of God's plan.

Of all God had given, she was man's gift.
God used man's body and formed her from his rib.

He created this woman to be his wife,
this is the reason God gave her life.

He said it's not good for man to be alone.
I'll give him woman to make him a home.

Flesh of his flesh and bone of his bone;
unlike any creature he has ever known.

And so we women are ordained to be wives.
Daughters of God for man by his side.

Not just a wife, a helpmeet and friend,
confidante, companion, from beginning to end.

A woman of virtue, love and grace.
A humble servant who knows her place.

We are to minister to our husband's needs.
With wisdom and kindness to help him succeed.

God loves us so much, He gave us instructions;
To live victorious and avoid destruction.

If we study the Bible we'll know His will,
Proverbs 31 tells the wife how to live.

The virtuous woman, wife, and mother;
serving her family and reaching out to others.

It's clear if we do this, our lives will be blessed;
if we do our part, then God can do the rest.

THE LITTLE THINGS

Those little things I do for you,
that make you happy I enjoy them, too.

No special occasion just let me know,
your love for me you want to show.

Doesn't have to cost much, a card or flower,
To remind me I'm your love, your heart's desire.

Doesn't take much to keep me pleased
A considerate thought, a kind deed.

There are times when all I'll need is you,
To love and support me in what I do.

True love is shown not in words but acts.
And the seeds we sow will all come back.

CHERISH YOUR LOVE

(To Ken and Pat)

As you enter into marriage with promises of love,
remember to cherish and honor this love.

For marriage is sacred, it's honorable, from God.
You must build on this marriage with a sincere heart.

It's not to be taken lightly as a fling or a toy.
There'll be days of tears and days of joy.

Give all that you have to this marriage, this gift.
Don't let others interfere or cause you to quit.

You're coming together as one, not two.
You must consider one another in all that you do.

Work hard in this marriage, it's required to grow,
and the blessings will blossom and happiness will flow.

Ken and Pat, you should cherish one another.
Always remember to keep God in your lives.

In the good times and bad times, he'll be right there
to love and keep you forever in His care!

SPECIAL TRIBUTES
Church & Pastoral

TRIBUTE TO ELDER ISAAC KING, JR.

(30th Pastoral Anniversary)

Pastor King is a blessing to us.
He's a great pastor and his job is tough.

Not only a Pastor, a psychologist too,
Social Worker and administrator to name a few.

Although he's busy carrying out his tasks,
he makes time in his schedule if you need him, just ask.

We're happy he's our pastor, he's also our friend;
to show our appreciation where do we begin?

30 years of service there is no measure
every second is valued, every minute a treasure.

Our love has grown from the very first day
and we thank God for choosing him to show us the way.

He's the example of how we should live;
to serve our Father, learning to give.

To love one another, one body, one accord;
praising and singing and glorifying the Lord.

God bless you, Pastor King
we want you to know
we hope you're with us for 30 years more!

TOUCH THE VISION

Remember the Vision God gave our Pastor;
See the Vision from God our Master.

Touch the vision, it's all around
for the goodness of God is so profound.

Look what He's done, His promises are true
Abundantly exceeding what we thought He would do

Behold His handiwork and don't forget
this is just the beginning
He's not through with us yet.

The vision may tarry but it surely will come.
What He has for us can be taken by no one.

Receive this gift from heaven above.
Cherish it, honor it, and use it in love.

Work together till the day is done.
Work in unity with love for everyone.

Obey God's Word so your blessings will grow.
For this house is the Lord's
and good seed must be sown.

God has given us an abundance of land
To work in His vineyard for the souls of man.

As a church, each member has a special part
Love and peace must be in our hearts.

Remember Pentecostal Temple, this Word from the Lord,
The blessings are greater when you're on one accord.

*A man shall receive nothing except it be
given him from heaven. John 2:17*

CELEBRATING THIRTY-EIGHT YEARS

He came to Inkster thirty eight years ago.
Didn't know how to pastor, never did it before.

He was patient and willing, a dedicated man,
His only credentials were a love for God,

A love for his people
and a humble obedience to carry out God's plan.

He was very young but he was not alone,
With a growing family he made Inkster his home.

A little white church on Harrison Street
had members who welcomed a pastor who'd teach.

God gave him this assignment he knows what we need.
And through this assignment many souls were freed.

There were many trials, so much to learn,
but God was there for every concern.

God molded him like a ball of clay
To make him the leader he is today.

Out of this assignment came a vision of love.
Encompassing the community
like a warm winter glove.

He's not in it for the money, glory or fame,
he's here to serve God and glorify his name.

Our pastor is a man who thinks of others before himself.
He lives by God's word, nothing less.

There have been many trials and many blessings
since that first day on Harrison Street.
The memories of those days and the saints are sweet.

Today we honor Pastor and Mrs. King
For those thirty eight years they served Pentecostal Temple.

We thank them again and we continue to pray
That many more blessings will come their way.

THE COINS

Once upon a time on Harrison Street
There was a family who kept the pastor's office neat.

They had a small boy to help them along
And while cleaning the office he noticed some coins.

It won't hurt to take a quarter or a dime
to buy some candy, the pastor won't mind.

Oh, that candy was so very, very good.
He remembered it throughout his childhood.

Many years have passed, not a word was said.
The pastor knew but he turned his head.

Today that boy has grown to a man.
He knows it was wrong and he has a plan.

He's paying it back every dime every cent
And he's paying with interest, all the money he spent.

So Pastor King just hold out your hand.
And receive this blessing, you're a wonderful man.

A TRIBUTE TO OUR FIRST LADY

It takes someone special to be a First Lady
someone caring, someone strong, someone loving, someone warm.

A person who shares and understands;
she's available, approachable, in great demand.

She supports her husband, she's virtuous and true,
whatever he needs, she's willing to do.

She's a pillar of strength, a priceless treasure;
her husband trusts her, his love is beyond measure.

It takes someone special to be a First Lady
someone kind, with busy hands,
laboring in God's kingdom, doing His commands.

She's reverenced and loved by those who know her;
she's a teacher, coordinator, role model, and counselor.

When I think of our First Lady, Margaret Jewel King,
I think of her smile and encouragement she brings.

And then I realize she's all of these things.
There's no other First Lady I'd rather call my own.
I know God sent her, she's our church cornerstone.

I'd like to thank her for all she's done,
I hope she realizes the many hearts she's won.

I pray God's blessings that she prosper and be in good health
continuing to grow---in God and in self.

I know our church will continue to be blessed
because our First Lady and Pastor are the very best!

OUR PASTORS

(Written for Debby Sims)

Our pastors are truly a blessing from God.
Committed and dedicated they work very hard.

I know God sent them to spread His word.
They glorify His name by the way they serve.

Anointed prophets loved by many.
With joy in their hearts and spirits of plenty.

They live a life that's holy and true.
Following Jesus as He told them to do.

God has anointed them in many ways.
In healing and deliverance they give Him praise.

The anointing of prosperity they also possess.
With a church that's growing, God's people are blessed.

As vessels of God they have helped many people,
the sick, downhearted, lame and feeble.

They are known and admired both near and far.
As for me, they hold a special place in my heart.

Today, I would like to express my love.
To let them know they are well thought of.

Pastors Wayne and Beverly
I cannot bless you with silver and gold.
I have no flowers for you to hold.

My heart is full of reverence for you,
for your love of God and His work that you do.

I pray god's blessings in all that you do,
that you continue to prosper in spiritual fruit.

I ask that you remember to pray for me,
that in God I'll be the best I can be.

May He always keep you in His care,
because there's no other like you anywhere.

A TRIBUTE TO PASTOR GAUDY

Elder Gaudy, our Pastor, dedicated and true.
From a small church his ministry grew.

He's gracious, caring, understanding and kind.
Cheerfully giving of his love, his time.

Whatever the problem he's willing to share.
He's never too busy, he's always there.

God chose him to pastor, Polk and Hall it began.
Thirty-six years many souls he would win.

His work as a pastor has become well known.
There are many who've learned
from the seeds He's sown.

God gave him a vision, it was in his plan,
to preach the gospel all over the land.

Not only at home, but other countries too,
helping the needy as we all should do.

We all are purposed by God to serve.
Some preach, some teach, to spread His word.

Elder Gaudy, our Pastor, our preacher and teacher,
leading, guiding, counseling God's people.

Sister Gaudy, his wife, a picture of pride.
Forever supporting him, by his side.

We love you Elder Gaudy, your first Lady too.
We pray for thirty-six more years with you.

TRIBUTES
FAMILY &
FRIENDS

A MARRIAGE BLESSING

Marriage is an expression of the love of God,
Created for man, direct from his heart

He ordained it, blessed it, planned it for us,
To glorify praise and lift Him up.

What does He say, what's His command?
What's His intention for the wedlock of man?

He who finds a wife finds a good thing God said.
I expect you to love her
cherish and protect her, you are the head.

She's bone of your bone and flesh of your flesh.
After Me, she's first, you must never forget.

This woman I've given you
because you prayed, you asked.
Teaching her and leading her, is now your task.

This husband I've given you is yours forever.
Love him, honor him. He is your treasure.

Krafus and Darlene, you know My name.
What you do for Me is never in vain.

Submit to one another. It's required not a choice.
The blessings flow when you obey My voice.

Others will be watching and I want them to see,
It's not about you, but all about Me.

FAMILY-GOD'S CREATION
(Newson Reunion)

When God created family He did it in love.
Unconditional, undying, everlasting love.

The love He gave us was to carry on
From family to family for generations to come.

Because God said man should not be alone,
He began with Adam and the family was born.

The family is so precious it can't be replaced.
The family structure is society's base.

Today with so many families in trouble,
We need to love, support, and encourage each other.

We must strive to keep our families together,
loving each other to make the world better.

A child needs his family for stability and strength,
To help him grow to be responsible and competent.

Our children grow up and have families of their own
But family reunions will bring them back home.

As we gather together, the first Newson reunion,
Rejoicing remembering, acquainting, playing,

We must remember the reason we're here.
We must remember it's worth the effort
To have our loved ones near.

We must remember God's plan
To endow His love into the family of man.

Remember our children, God's gift to us
Remember our parents, God's loan to us

Remember we must always be loving and strong
And never forget God
For He promised we'd never be alone.

MOTHER

Tribute to my Mom

Mother can mean many things to us.
To me a mother is love and trust.

Our lives are based on what we learn from mother.
Her place is to guide us, teach us and love us.

She gave us life through God, His vessel.
Her love is strong, warm, and special.

Even a baby in mother's arms
knows a feeling of peace, he's safe from harm.

A mother is there when we take our first breath.
She's with us when there is no one else.

She's a pillar of strength, the family backbone,
whatever the need, she takes care of home.

My mother is warm, loving and kind.
I can call on her at any time.

She's the kind of mother who's always there,
willing to give, ready to share.

What is this love God gave to mother?
It's beyond compare, it's like no other.

Thank you mother for the sacrifices you've made,
the love you gave, the prayers you prayed.

I love and appreciate everything you've done,
when it comes to mothers, you're number one!

PORTRAIT OF A FATHER

A tribute to my Dad

My Father is a man with a great love for family.
He's caring, kind, and understanding.

The love he has is from the depths of his soul.
From the time he was a child, a family was his goal.

He had visions and dreams of the things he would do.
Though some were not realized, some did come true.

This man who is my father stands up for his beliefs.
He makes known his feelings,
they're conscientious and deep.

He has a strong conviction for helping others,
whether neighbor, friend, sister or brother.

When it comes to his children, they are his treasure.
Any time with them brings him pleasure.

Whatever they need, there's no hesitation.
He'll be there for them without reservation.

Grandchildren, cooking, and gardening he enjoys;
and he loves traveling south to the place he was born.

My dad is a man who's one of a kind.
A more loving father one could never find.

All of my life, he's been there for me;
supporting and comforting me whenever the need.

Close to my heart and with love and respect,
he's a part of my life I'll treasure till death.

A RETIREMENT OF HONOR

Retirement is a time we look forward to, we pursue.
It's a time in our lives we can choose what to do.

Jerry it's your time, you've paid your dues.
You've worked hard, you've been faithful,
and you've been honest and true.

Many years have come and gone.
Through the ups and downs you've remained strong.

I've watched you grow into a fine young man,
and in times of trouble, you took a stand.

You had standards and you wouldn't back down.
You are a person who will stand your ground.

The tragedies of life were a daily routine,
as a police officer through dangers unseen.

As an officer of the law you were sworn to serve,
You were willing and ready to protect and preserve.

Through the years you've endured some pain,
But God has brought you through the sunshine and rain.

You've closed the door on this chapter of your life
And a new door opens, no stress, less strife.

Your time is now, you're retired, and you're free
Though circumstances looked grim, it's better you'll agree.

When God answers prayers, He does everything well.
His love comforts us and our fears He dispels.

As my brother, I admire you, love you, and respect you.
You're an upstanding citizen, brother, father, son and friend.
You're someone on whom we all can depend.

As we gather here to celebrate you,
I know you'll succeed in whatever you do!

Always remember to put God first,
He'll keep you and guide you.
You won't hunger or thirst.

I wish you happiness and all good things.
I wish you the best that retirement can bring.

AN HONOR OF ACCOMPLISHMENT

Today, I honor my brother on a promotion
and accomplishment in life.
He was determined to do something positive
and determined to do it right.

Jerry, as a brother, you've always been there for me.
As a child you were special and a gift to me.

As a man, you are honorable and a source of pride to me.
This day is very special because you're also a part of me.

When God created this family, He knew just what to do.
He saved a special place, created just for you.

I have a place, my sisters have theirs, as well as father and mother,
but your place is reserved especially for brothers.

Looking back on the day you were born,
you were exactly what I had asked.

It was an exciting and happy time,
I had a brother at last!

I remember the days when you were small.
The things you would do I'll always recall.

Mischievous things that made me blue,
but now I know you were just being you.

As your sister and friend I look up to you in pride,
not only because I love you, but in you I can confide.

I've watched you grow from a child to a man.
Each goal you've completed
and have now achieved another;

You're DEPUTY CHIEF OF POLICE!
I thank God that you're my brother
and that He's protected you from harm.
I can't imagine life without you, your love, your humor and charm.

I love the family gatherings, the memories and laughter we share.
I would never trade you for another, anytime, anywhere.

So today, as friends and family are gathered in celebration,
I pray God's continuous blessings, and a great big
CONGRATULATIONS!

MY BEST FRIEND IS GETTING MARRIED

Written for Debby to Jocelyn

My best friend is getting married and it's time to celebrate.
I remember the days when we were small,
we dreamed about this day.

Our friendship has lasted over 30 years,
we've formed a very close bond.

Although our lives took separate paths
we never lost touch, we'd correspond.

For seven long years we were miles apart,
though separated by distance, but never in heart.

We both met Jesus the very same year,
though in different cities, our God was near.

A true friend is rare; to have one you're blessed.
I can truly say Jocelyn is among the very best.

When I think of her personality I have to smile sometimes.
She's hyper, bubbly, SUPER emotional,
the most caring person you'll find.

She's tasteful, warm, a strong woman of God;
she never changes, she's the same all the time.

Soon she'll share her life with Kenny, the man she loves,
her Isaac, her prince, the one she dreamed of.

I pray she'll be happy and ALWAYS in love,
that she'll keep her bubbly personality
and God's blessings from above.

PEGGY

To Peggy Jordan

God created each of us and made everyone special.
And when He came to Peggy, He made her extra special.

He made her strong to overcome adversity and pain.
And when the trials come, she never complains.

He made her with a spirit so sweet and kind.
The most loving person you will ever find.

He gave her compassion and concern for others.
She's faithful dependable, considerate, trustworthy.

Whatever you need she's there for you;
doing all she can to see you through.

God made her patient and very understanding.
Always encouraging, never demanding.

There's so much about Peggy I admire and adore.
She's a wonderful mother, wife, daughter and more.

She's a beautiful person with a heart of gold
a smile and personality that touches your soul.

She's extra special and takes life in stride.
Giving and sharing not filled with pride.

Peggy, you're such a blessing,
an example of love and peace

I thank God that you are in my life,
may your blessings never cease.

BIRTHDAY TRIBUTE
To Latral Austin

Celebration and love is the reason we're here
To honor a loved one so sweet and dear.

Fifty years ago Latral Walker entered this world
God had blessed the Walker family with another baby girl.

Anointed to sing and bring glory to God
This child would sing, and sing from her heart.

As she grew it was evident she possessed a great love
A love that would pour out in her profession as a nurse.

Along the way she married and became a mother of three
Raising them to love God to trust Him and believe.

Many times she struggled to reach her goal
But she raised her children, just her and the Lord.

She's watched them grow, she's watched them mature
You can see the respect, the love, they are secure.

Fifty years encompass many steps, many miles
But God has kept her, she is His child.

His purpose for her is evident today
As a mother she is admired for the great job she's done
As a nurse she's experienced, loving and warm.

She sings so sweet you know it's a gift
It touches your soul your spirit, it lifts.

We're so blessed to have Latral in our lives.
A very special person, a source of godly pride.

We honor God with Latral in celebrating her birth.
For the godly example she displays here on earth.

As God showers you with blessings, may you continue to grow,
As you bask in His <u>Son</u>shine and others see your glow.

As you embark upon another fifty years of life
Growing in His grace blossoming in Christ.

May your pathways be smooth, and your sorrows few.
We pray God's blessings continually for you.

May His hand guide you in all that you do;
And His blood cover you whatever you go through.

We celebrate the joy, the peace, the love.
That's bestowed on you from heaven above.

Let this be a day you will never forget.
And may this birthday be the best one yet!

BIRTHDAY LOVE

To Ethel Jordan

There's love in the house flowing inside out.
And it's all for you Ethel, there is no doubt!

Today is special, it's a blessing too;
as we gather together to celebrate you.

A woman of virtue, loving and sweet,
with a beautiful smile for everyone you meet.

Born on this day a few years ago.
God has blessed you with a youthful glow.

We're thankful Ethel that you're a part of our lives.
You're never self-serving but giving and wise.

You're aunt, mother, grandmother, sister and friend
You're so special to us, where do I begin?

When it comes to shopping, any mall will do.
You like shopping with your daughters for an outfit or two.

And we know your favorite color is red.
The shopping's not done without a hat for your head.

Your love for your family cannot be denied.
Your children bless you and honor you,
and look on you with pride.

Surprise was their goal and they worked very hard.
They wanted to do more than a gift and a card.

To see your face filled with happiness and joy;
creating beautiful memories you never had before.

So as we laugh, have fun, and celebrate your day,
may many more blessings come your way.

We pray this birthday is the best one yet.
A day filled with happiness that you'll never forget!

OUR MOTHER

Written for Betty Rozier to her mother

Mothers are beautiful like a flower.
With a special fragrance and a unique power.

This power for love, a special heart,
a love for her children that will not depart.

Though mothers may be different
God's purpose is the same;
to nurture her children
and comfort them in pain.

Our mother is caring, wise and warm.
A woman of stature and full of charm.

She's conscientious, kind, she knows how to dress.
When it comes to cooking, she's the best.

Housekeeping, finance, she made a way.
Stretching a dollar so every bill would be paid.

There were times when she felt she was all alone,
but she continued to sacrifice for her children, her home.

She taught her daughters everything she knew
So they could be strong and self sufficient too.

Like the woman in Proverbs going about her tasks,
taking care of her family, remaining steadfast.

A virtuous woman, she passed the test,
her children rise up and call her blessed.

Emma Rozier, your children bless you today;
the love you gave, sacrifices
you've made could never be repaid.

Because it's your birthday, a time to celebrate,
a time to reflect, honor, and appreciate.

To let you know we love you and we care
and there's no mother like you anywhere!

MY LORD, MY SISTER, MYSELF
Reflections of a Retreat

The Lord has blessed me in so many ways.
He brought me to this retreat today.

I'm blessed with two sisters we're bound by blood.
But I'm blessed with three others, bound through His love.

We've been sisters for many years.
We've shared laughter, joy and tears.

Our bond is strong, our friendship rare.
The Lord has shown us how to love and care.

The retreat is one way He lets us know,
He has many ways for us to learn and grow.

Today we've met new sisters in Christ
To love, share and enhance our lives.

The retreat has inspired me, I've learned many things,
And I'll always remember what sisterhood means.

THE LOVE OF MOTHER

Written for Sherry Neal to her mother

There's something special about the love of mother,
a gift from God unlike any other.

As I look back when I was small,
I knew on mother I could always call.

No matter what time of day or night,
Mother was there to make things right.

A mother is someone more precious than gold,
a shoulder to cry on, a hand to hold;

a heart full of love, she's patient and kind;
always willing to share her time.

I owe all I am to my mother today;
she guided and counseled me and taught me to pray.

I love you Jean Lawson; this poem is for you;
for a Mother's Day that's special,
and a heart that's true!

IN LOVING MEMORY

MOMMA WE'RE GOING TO MISS YOU

To my mother

Momma we're going to miss you so much.
Your smiling face, your loving touch.

We'll miss your voice when you call our names.
We know our lives will never be the same.

You were always there praying for us.
You taught us in Jesus we should always trust.

Whatever the situation, large or small,
You said on Jesus we should always call.

He loaned you to us and He's called you home
You're with Him now, you'll never be alone.

It made you so happy to pray for others.
There are many who love you and call you mother.

Oh momma, we'll miss you so,
But in our hearts we know you must go.

You've touched many lives with your loving ways,
The sacrifices you made can never be repaid.

We thank God for blessing us with a mother like you,
No one could love us more than you do.

We can't touch you, hug you or kiss you any more.
Your love will remain with us forever.

We cherish your memory and we know right now,
You're at peace, you're happy in a place that's better.

MOTHER GIBSON

A woman of character, strength and grace,
so many memories that can't be erased.

Her love for people reached far and wide,
drawing others to her as she touched their lives.

Whatever the need it was never too much,
reaching out to others with a loving touch.

Generous and kind she labored hard,
displaying the love she had for God.

She always had an encouraging word;
never too busy, ready to serve.

Programs, dinners, fundraising events,
Mother Gibson was there to raise every cent.

We're going to miss Mother Gibson,
her warmth, her smile.
but God said, it's time to go my child.

I want you here, your work is done,
your trials are over, your race is won.

I love you more than anyone could,
I've prepared a place for you
that's beautiful and good.

Mother Gibson left a legacy of generosity and love,
something we can cherish and be proud of.

Though we can't touch her or seek her advice,
her memory will always be a part of our lives.

TRACY

To Gloria, loss of her daughter

There aren't many words to ease your pain
I know life for you will never be the same.

Take comfort in knowing we love you and we care
and though I'm not with you physically, spiritually I'm there.

When God blesses us with children, they're here for a while.
Entrusted in our care, His precious child.

God blessed you with Tracy, she was here on loan,
Now He has decided to call her home.

She's quietly resting in His loving arms,
free from pain, suffering and harm.

As a mother I feel your pain; I feel your anguish, too.
But know I care, and understand, I'm praying for you.

Sometimes we ask why, but only God knows,
His purpose, His plan for our lives, our souls.

Because I know Jesus resides in your heart,
and His love for you will never depart.

I know you'll find comfort and His abiding peace
and the memories of Tracy you'll forever keep.

WAYMAN

Wayman was considerate, caring and kind.
When it came to helping others he didn't mind.

He was here with us for only a short while.
He shared his love, his life, his smile.

He enjoyed his family his love was strong
but God said it's time to call Wayman home.

His son and daughter held the key to his heart;
his best friend was Charlie and they were seldom apart.

He loved playing baseball his wife kept score.
He played as a Pro some years before.

Though Wayman's not here, his memories remain
his love is carried on in his family and his name.

REMEMBERING WAYMAN

To Gwen, loss of her husband

A faithful companion, husband and friend.
You thought you'd be together until the end.

You miss him more than anyone knows.
You see him in your children
as you watch them grow.

It takes so long for the pain to heal.
But trust in God, He's here, He's real.

Life is like a merry-go-round.
Sometimes up and sometimes down.

But through it all God is there.
He's able to handle every care.

Your faith in God will keep you strong
With God in your life, you can't go wrong.

Just trust in Him to lead and guide you.
As your memories of Wayman
are instilled inside you.

Through every trial that you go through
God will keep and comfort you.

In His love, His peace will come.
So be assured you're never alone.

DIANE

Diane, you're a woman who lived her faith.
An example of strength, beauty and grace.

You loved to read and share what you learned;
As a teacher you cared, you were concerned.

You were proud of your heritage, it was important to you.
Always searching in the books you read
for knowledge of your history, knowledge of the truth.

A person of character, unique and sweet.
You fought long and hard, never accepting defeat.

You're an example of courage, always trusted in God.
Never giving up, you stood… with love in your heart.

You're like a flower whose time has come
you've been plucked from the garden
but your fragrance lingers on.

Like the words of a song with a sweet melody,
Your message of faith leaves a strong legacy.

Your time with us was not very long
and you touched our lives like the warm morning sun.

We'll miss your presence but your memories remain.
We have comfort in knowing you're no longer in pain.

We have comfort in knowing you're safe in God's arms.
Free from pain, free from harm.

Though we can't touch you or hug you, you live in our hearts
and the memories we have will never depart.

Rest Diane, in God's prepared place,
where you can worship, love, and behold Him, face to face.

A TRIBUTE TO JOAN BUTLER

The time has come and you must go.
The mysteries of life, we do not know.

But I know God gave you to my children and me to love.
As grandmother to my children and mother-in-law to me,
you leave a legacy of love and history.

When I needed support, you were there.
With a listening ear you showed you care.

As time went on, our relationship grew.
I cherished the friendship I found in you.

You fought a good fight, the battle was hard.
And now you're at peace in the arms of God.

Joan we'll miss you and the times we shared.
The talks, the laughter and joy we had.

The memories of you I'll always treasure,
they'll forever be in my heart.

You've touched my life in a way
that could never be forgotten.

I know someday I'll see you again.
Your smiling face, your outstretched hand.

But until then, my mother-in-law, my friend,
my love for you will never end.

ANDRE

Andre so special, intelligent and sweet.
Like a beautiful flower you left a fragrance
Of a love so strong, it will never cease.

You touched our lives like no one could.
Though with us only for a while.

Now you've gone to be with God.
He loves you more, you're His child.

When we think of you we see a man
who loves to cook and work with his hands.

When we think of you we see someone
who's kind, dependable, a caring son.

When we think of you we see a man
who's willing to help.

Putting others first when there's a need
and forgetting about himself.

When we think of you we see many things;
nephew, cousin, grandson, friend.

We carry your love within our hearts
and it will never, ever end.

Rest Andre in God's loving arms.
Free from pain, free from harm.

NOTABLE MIX

WATCH YOUR WORDS

Are you aware of the power you possess in the words you speak?
Words can build up or tear down. The Bible warns us about the
power of the tongue. If you want to know what the tongue can do,
the books of Proverbs and James provide much detail on the tongue.

Death and life are in the power of the tongue
Proverbs 18:21

A wholesome tongue is a tree of life
Proverbs 15:4

But no man can tame the tongue. It is an unruly evil full of deadly poison.
James 3:8

We can destroy or build up with the words we speak. Every man,
woman and child has this awesome power. We must be careful not
to abuse it. God wants us to use this power to edify and heal. If we
speak without thinking, we can cause a great deal of harm. However,
if we allow the Holy Spirit to guide us and be slow to speak and quick
to hear, we will use this power in the manner God intended. Use
your power to edify and encourage someone today.

MAKING A DIFFERENCE STARTS WITH ME

Do you see a need for change in your life or environment? Are you distressed by what's going on around you? Realize that you can make a difference. God has a plan for our lives and each one of us is unique with different gifts and talents.

The first step to making a difference begins with a desire and a decision to seek change. It has been said that the room for improvement is the biggest room in the house. Taking an assessment of ourselves, the workplace, home and community will reveal many opportunities for change and development.

 Considering the problems of society today, there is something everyone can do to make it better. The gifts God placed in us are to be used and shared to help others. Giving of ourselves in time, finances, sharing of knowledge, visiting the sick, even a smile or word of encouragement can make someone's day. Whatever you do, it may be large or small. If helps another, the difference you've made can encourage your brother.

EMBRACING CHANGE

Change…what does that word mean to you? Webster says change is to become different or to pass from one phase to another, to undergo transformation. How do you view change? No matter how we feel about change, it impacts each one of us in one way or another but it's our attitude that determines whether it becomes a positive or negative experience. Some people just do not like any type of change, refuse to accept it and will fight it all the way. When we accept and embrace change and realize that we can benefit and grow, we open the door to opportunities that may not have been available before. We open the door to greatness and success.

Take a moment to think about the changes taking place in your life. What is your attitude about change? I've learned that even when it's negative you can pull a positive out of the experience if you look hard enough. Change is constant. Expect it, grow in it, and embrace it!

THE SEEDS YOU SOW

The seeds you sow you truly will reap.
Whether laughter and joy or sorrow and grief.

This life of yours is not for you.
It's to glorify God through the good deeds you do.

It's important to God that we love one another.
He is our Father and we're sisters and brothers.

To give of yourself is God's desire.
Through good times and bad, through tests and trials.

He knows in this world there is so much need
And you are His vessel for planting good seed.

It's not about you but God alone.
He rules and reigns from heaven's throne.

He sits high and He has a plan
He watches and judges the deeds of man.

So whatever you do, sow seeds of love
To reap a harvest from heaven above.

JUDGE NOT

When we judge or make assumptions about someone, there is a danger of error in that assumption. We do this without considering the consequences of our actions. Many times circumstances may cause a person to act a certain way so that they will not portray some pain or negative situation they are experiencing in their lives. He or she could be internalizing some issues that would cause negative behavior. We as outsiders may form an opinion or make a judgment without knowing all of the facts and cause resentment and hostility or more pain; especially when it is an incorrect assumption.

When making judgments or assumptions are we being self righteous, thinking more highly of ourselves than we should? When faced with a situation that provides an opportunity to make assumptions or judgments, we must be careful, open minded and concerned about others. We must remember it is always possible that we could be in the same or similar situations. Most of all, we should remember we do not have the right to judge others. We need to examine ourselves because no one is perfect.

So as we go about our day to day living, we should be willing to forgive, have a concern for others and be open minded. And most of all - leave the judging for God. It's His responsibility.

TEAMWORK SPELLS SUCCESS

Someone once said that the word team means…

Together
Everyone
Achieves
More

Team players are individuals who work together to accomplish a task.
To support one another when there's a need and when asked.

The focus is not on the individual, but on the task itself.
Personalities can't become obstacles because the goal must be kept.

When everyone works together and tasks are matched to skills,
the burden is shared, the project is manageable and easier to fulfill.

When this occurs, there is much less stress
leading the project to a desirable success.

LOOKING TO RETIREMENT

We all look forward to that special day.
When we can retire and go home to stay.

Won't have to get up, no clock to punch.
Won't have to run back from break and lunch.

In the book of our lives we turn the page.
As in opening night we walk on stage.

An exciting time with an unknown future.
Looking ahead to a time of renewal.

Yes, retirement is a time we look to enjoy.
Living our lives unlike before.

A time of anticipation yet a hint of reservation.
An unknown future can bring concern and hesitation.

This is a time when we activate our faith,
Giving all to God because He's good, He's great.

We'll have memories of times that can't be erased;
the good times and bad all have their place.

As we retire, leaving friends behind,
The relationships we formed are one of a kind.

We must cherish each day and make every minute count,
Giving thanks to God because He brought us out!

About the Author

Nadine Flowers grew up in a small suburb of Detroit. She is a graduate of William Tyndale College and has a Bachelor's degree in Business Administration. She is currently employed at Blue Cross Blue Shield of Michigan as an Audit Analyst. She is currently a member Christian Tabernacle Church in Southfield, Michigan where Dr. James L. Morman is her pastor.

She was a member of Pentecostal Temple C.O.G.I.C. located in Inkster, Michigan for many years where she continues to have many friends and family.

She is the mother of two adult daughters, Sherice and Nataki. She feels God has called her to minister and encourage women and is currently studying to become a Certified Biblical Counselor through the Christian Research and Development Program. She is also a member of Christian Women for Change, a newly birthed ministry, inspired and led by the Holy Spirit, called to minister to others and change lives based on the Word of God.

She believes God placed gifts in each one of us and aspires to walk in the gifts and calling God has placed on her life. She desires to develop these gifts to be used as God intended and obey His calling in order to give Him glory.

For more information contact:
Nadine Flowers
c/o PriorityONE Publications
P.O. Box 725 ▪ Farmington, MI 48332
Phone: 800-331-8841 ▪ Email: nflowers@p1pubs.com

In Him I Live!

By Nadine Flowers

Name _____

Address _____

City _____State _____ Zip _____

Phone _____Fax _____

Email _____

Quantity	
Price *(each)*	**$12.99**
Subtotal	
S & H *(each)*	**$2.99**
MI Tax 6%	
TOTAL	

METHOD OF PAYMENT:

☐ Check or Money Order (***Make payable to:*** **PriorityONE Publications**)

☐ Visa   ☐ Master Card   ☐ American Express

Acct No. _____

Expiration Date (*mm/yy*) _____

Signature _____

Mail your payment with this form to:
PriorityONE Publications
P. O. Box 725
Farmington, MI 48332
(800) 331-8841 – Toll Free
(313) 893-3359 – Southeast Michigan
URL: http://www.p1pubs.com
Email: info@p1pubs.com

Printed in the United States
111263LV00003B/52-165/P